WRJC

W9-BIR-512

THE STORY OF
Christmas

By Barbara Cooney
Illustrated by Loretta Krupinski

HarperCollinsPublishers

The text for this book was first published in *Christmas*, a Crowell Holiday Book edited by Susan Bartlett Weber, written and illustrated by Barbara Cooney, copyright ©1967 by Barbara Cooney.

The illustrations in this book were painted with gouache and colored pencils on sabretooth paper.

THE STORY OF CHRISTMAS

CHRISTMAS! Everywhere people are getting ready for Christmas.

Behind closed doors children are planning surprises.

Delicious things are cooking in the kitchen.

Houses and churches are trimmed with green boughs.

Candles are lit.

Eyes shine.

People sing.

The days are cold. The nights are long. But the air is full of magic and anticipation.

Around the world children are waiting impatiently to celebrate the birthday of a little Jewish boy. He was born long ago, in a faraway village, in a stable. His name was Jesus of Nazareth.

When Jesus grew up, he became a great and wise teacher. He taught people to love God and to love each other. His teachings became the worldwide religion called Christianity. It is Jesus' birthday that we call Christmas.

Jesus was born nearly two thousand years ago in the country of Palestine. The story of his birth is written in the New Testament of the Bible. It is called the story of the Nativity.

Palestine, the home of the Jewish people, was then part of the huge Roman Empire, ruled by an Emperor. Not long before Jesus was born, the Emperor decided to count the people in his Empire. He ordered each house-holder to return to his hometown to be counted.

In the village of Nazareth lived a carpenter named Joseph and his young wife Mary. Even though Mary was soon to have a baby, she went with Joseph to the town where he had been born. The town, Bethlehem, was far to the south. It was a long, weary journey to get there.

When they reached Bethlehem, the streets were crowded with people who had come to be counted. The inn was full. The only place for Mary to rest was a stable. And while they were in Bethlehem, Mary's baby was born. For want of a cradle, she laid her son, wrapped in swaddling clothes, in the cattle's manger.

That same night shepherds were watching their sheep in the country outside of Bethlehem when suddenly the fields were lit with a bright and dazzling light. The shepherds became frightened. But angels appeared and told them that a Savior had been born. They would find the baby wrapped in swaddling clothes, lying in a manger.

After the angels had disappeared, the shepherds hurried to Bethlehem. There, in the stable, they found the baby Jesus.

A great star hung in the sky that night. Far off in the east there were Wise Men who saw it. They thought it was a sign that the Messiah, a new leader, had been born. And so, bearing gifts, they followed the star.

The Wise Men followed the star until it came to rest over the stable in Bethlehem. They knelt before the baby Jesus. In front of him they placed their gifts of gold and frankincense and myrrh. People believe that the Wise Men arrived in Bethlehem twelve days after Jesus was born, on Twelfth Night, sometimes called Epiphany.

Today, families all over the world celebrate Jesus' birthday on December twenty-fifth, but in many countries the celebrations begin before Christmas Day and last until Twelfth Night. On Twelfth Night, the holiday season ends.

To celebrate in December is an old, old custom. Long before the birth of Jesus there were midwinter festivals. When the long December nights began to grow shorter and the days started to grow longer, people celebrated the rebirth of the sun. These people, called pagans, worshipped the sun.

The peasants in northern Europe had a feast called Yule. A huge Yule log was brought in from the woods. As a symbol of the sun, it was blessed and burned with much ceremony.

During the Yule season the gray-bearded Norse god Odin was supposed to wander among his people. He came to reward and punish as he saw fit. He wore a blue cloak and a wide-brimmed hat pulled down over his one eye.

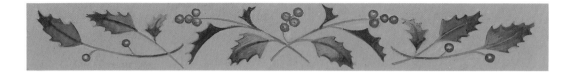

The ancient Romans had a December festival, too, the Saturnalia. It was named after Saturn, the Roman god of agriculture. It celebrated the return of the sun, as well as the rich harvest. A mock king, called Saturn like the god, was chosen to rule over the merrymakers during the festival.

The Saturnalia was a holiday for everyone. Schools were closed. Shops were shut. Houses and temples were decorated with green boughs and holly branches.

People dressed up in costumes and danced and feasted. They gave each other gifts of wax fruit, candles, and dolls.

Everyone enjoyed these December celebrations, including the first Christians. But the Church did not approve of pagan customs that belonged to a time before the coming of Jesus. The Christians, however, did not want to give them up.

Five hundred years after Jesus was born, the Church decided to celebrate Jesus' birthday in December. In this way, many of the merry pagan customs became part of the Christmas festival.

Over the years King Saturn of the Saturnalia became the Lord of Misrule. During the Middle Ages, the Lord of Misrule reigned during the Christmas season. In the castles and palaces there was gaiety and feasting while he was lord.

Odin's place was filled by St. Nicholas, another mysterious old man who came to reward good children. The first St. Nicholas was a kind and generous bishop who lived in the fourth century. Later this bishop became the patron saint of children.

St. Nicholas, riding a white pony, still visits children in Holland, Belgium, Switzerland, and parts of Austria and Germany.

Today, in the United States, we have Santa Claus. He is a white-bearded, round, and jolly little man who lives at the North Pole. There he and his helpers work all year making toys.

On Christmas Eve, when all are asleep, Santa Claus sets out with his bulging sack of toys. He flies over the rooftops in a sleigh drawn by eight reindeer. With a clattering of hooves, the reindeer halt on the housetops. Santa Claus alights. Then down the chimney he comes to fill the stockings of the children with toys and sweets. Santa also leaves presents under the Christmas tree.

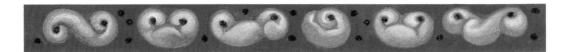

Since pagan times the mid-December festival has been a festival of fire and light. At Christmastime the Yule log is still burned in northern Europe. Torches and bonfires are lit in many countries. Fireworks are set off in Italy, France, and Spain. Candlelight services are held in many Christian churches on Christmas Eve. Candles shine in the windows and on the altars.

In Sweden the first day of the Christmas season is called St. Lucia's Day. Before dawn the eldest daughter in the family delivers coffee and cakes to her family in bed. She wears a white dress with a red sash, and on her head rests a crown of lighted candles.

Candles glow in windows, too. Lights shine on Christmas trees. Fire and light, once symbols of the sun god, now serve to brighten the way of the Christ Child.

We, too, use greens as did the ancient Romans. We decorate our houses with evergreens and holly. We put wreaths on our doors, and hang mistletoe overhead.

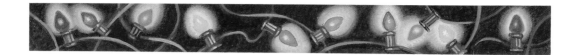

The tradition of Christmas trees began in medieval Germany with an evergreen decorated with red apples. Later decorations included fruits and nuts, paper roses, lighted candles, painted eggshells, and candy. German settlers put up the first Christmas trees in the United States in the early 1800s. The star that often tops the tree represents the star that guided the Wise Men to Jesus' stable in Bethlehem. Today, we trim our Christmas trees with electric lights, candy canes, tinsel, and brightly colored ornaments.

Christmas is a time to think of others. As during Saturnalia, friends are remembered and grudges forgotten. We send cards to our friends and wish them a merry Christmas.

For the people we love best, we buy or make presents. We tie them up in bright papers with shiny ribbons. Then, on Christmas Day or on Christmas Eve, the packages are opened beside the Christmas tree.

We also feast and make merry. From kitchens come the good odors of Christmas cakes and cookies, and roasting turkeys or geese.

At this happy time of year we sing songs of rejoicing, called carols, in churches and homes and in the streets.

In schools and churches children put on pageants and plays that tell the story of the first Christmas.

Scenes, called crèches, show figures of the shepherds and the Wise Men gathered around the holy family.

Over the years legends have been added to the Christmas story. We suppose that Mary rode a donkey on her way to Bethlehem, though the Bible does not tell us so.

The Wise Men are sometimes called the three kings. The Bible does not say how many Wise Men there were. But the legends tell of three, named Caspar, Melchior, and Balthazar. Some say the Wise Men came on camels; others say on horses.

An ox and an ass, it is said, were in the stable with the holy family. Their breath kept Jesus warm.

Sometimes we hear of other animals. One is the lamb who gave his wool for Jesus' blanket. Another is the little wren who brought moss and feathers to line the Christ Child's bed. There is the raven who flew over the stable that first Christmas Eve. He was the first creature to know of Jesus' birth. And there is the cock who crowed all that night till dawn.

Many people believe that Jesus was born at midnight. Each Christmas Eve, at this magic hour, animals, they say, kneel to worship and are given the power of human speech.

Animals play such an important part in the Christmas legend that they are treated with special kindness at Christmas. In some countries the cattle and horses are given extra fodder. In Poland they share with the family the bread served at the Christmas feast. In Scandinavia a sheaf of grain is tied to the top of a tall pole as a feast for the birds. Handfuls of grain are strewn for them across the tops of walls and on rooftops.

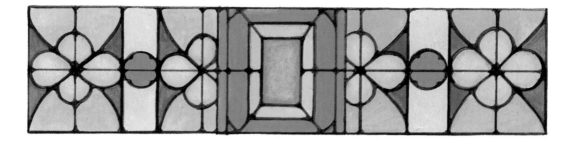

There are different customs in every country. But on Christmas Eve and on Christmas Day, services are held in churches everywhere. And at midnight the church bells ring out so that people will know that it is Christmas Day.

At Christmastime we decorate our houses. We exchange gifts. We feast and make merry, just as people did long before Jesus was born. But the heart of the winter festival called Christmas is the Christmas story. It is the story of a little boy who was born long ago, in a faraway village, in a stable.

Things to Make at Christmastime

Rolled Christmas Cookies

INGREDIENTS:

1 cup (2 sticks) butter,
    softened
¾ cup sugar
1 egg
2 tablespoons milk
½ teaspoon vanilla

⅛ teaspoon lemon extract
    (optional)
3 cups flour
1 teaspoon baking
    powder
½ teaspoon salt

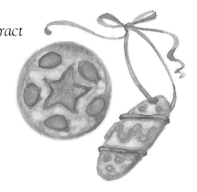

DECORATIONS: *sour balls of varying colors*

In a large bowl, cream the butter until smooth. Gradually add the sugar and continue to cream. Add the egg, milk, vanilla, and lemon extract. Beat well. Blend dry ingredients together in a bowl and add to batter. (If dough is too sticky to handle, refrigerate for 30 minutes.) Roll on floured surface a third at a time to ⅛" thickness. Cut freehand or with cookie cutters and place on a cookie sheet. You can bake the cookies as they are or decorate them using either method described on the next page. In any case, they should bake at 350°F for 10 to 12 minutes. To use them as decorations, just poke a hole in cookies before baking, then string with ribbon to hang on the tree. Or you can insert a small hairpin to hang the cookies.

You can turn your cookies into stained glass windows:
Using a blender or food processor, crush several sour balls of each color, keeping colors separate. Place cookies on a foil-covered cookie sheet. Using a small, sharp knife, cut out shapes inside each cookie to make a stained glass pattern. Fill holes just to the top with crushed candy pieces. While cooking, watch carefully so candy does not turn brown. Cool completely on sheets. Peel away foil.

You can also decorate your cookies with colored frosting.

CLOVE-COVERED ORANGE

To make this great-smelling holiday decoration, you'll need:

1 orange
box of cloves
3 feet of red ribbon

2 straight pins
scissors

Push clove stems into the outside of an orange until peel is completely covered. Cut ribbon into 2 unequal pieces with one piece an inch or two longer than the other. Wrap the shorter piece of ribbon around the covered orange and pin

both ends firmly at the top. Cut off excess ribbon. Then give the orange a quarter turn and repeat with the longer piece of ribbon, also pinning at the top. With leftover ribbon, tie a loop for hanging.

 ## PINE CONE BIRD FEEDER

Decorate for Christmas outside your home and give the birds a treat by making a pine cone bird feeder out of the following:

large pine cone *1 cup sunflower seeds or bird seed*
roughly 18 inches of red or green yarn *butter knife*
1/2–3/4 cup peanut butter *sheet of waxed paper*

Tie yarn securely to the top of the pine cone. Using the knife, generously coat the pine cone with peanut butter. Then pour the sunflower seeds or bird seed onto a sheet of waxed paper. Roll the pine cone in the seed until the peanut-buttery spots are completely covered. (You may need to use your fingers to sprinkle on extra seed and push it in.) Tie the bird feeder onto a tree branch and watch the birds feast on their Christmas treat!